Mashed Potatoes and Davey

by Megan Orr

D1520475

Baker's Plays
7611 Sunset Blvd.
Los Angeles, CA 90042
bakersplays.com

NOTICE

This book is offered for sale at the price quoted only on the understanding that, if any additional copies of the whole or any part are necessary for its production, such additional copies will be purchased. The attention of all purchasers is directed to the following: this work is fully protected under the copyright laws of the United States of America, the British Commonwealth, including Canada, and all other countries of the Copyright Union. Violations of the Copyright Law are punishable by fine or imprisonment, or both. The copying or duplication of this work or any part of this work, by hand or by any process, is an infringement of the copyright and will be vigorously prosecuted.

This play may not be produced by amateurs or professionals for public or private performance without first submitting application for performing rights. Licensing fees are due on all performances whether for charity or gain, or whether admission is charged or not. Since performance of this play without the payment of the Licensing fees renders anybody participating liable to severe penalties imposed by the law, anybody acting in this play should be sure, before doing so, that the Licensing fees has been paid. Professional rights, reading rights, radio broadcasting, television and all mechanical rights, etc. are strictly reserved. Application for performing rights should be made directly to BAKER'S PLAYS.

No one shall commit or authorize any act or omission by which the copyright of, or the right to copyright, this play may be impaired. No one shall make any changes in this play for the purpose of production.

Publication of this play does not imply availability for performance. Both amateurs and professionals considering a production are strongly advised in their own interest to apply to Baker's Plays for written permission before starting rehearsals, advertising, or booking a theatre.

Whenever the play is produced, the author's name must be carried in all publicity, advertising and programs. Also, the following notice must appear on all printed programs, "Produced by special arrangement with Baker's Plays."

Licensing fees for MASHED POTATOES AND DAVEY are based on a per performance rate and payable one week in advance of the production.

Please consult the Baker's Plays website at www.bakersplays.com or our current print catalogue for up to date licensing fee information.

MASHED POTATOES AND DAVEY
ISBN **978-0-87440-245-2**
#2058-B

MASHED POTATOES AND DAVEY was first performed on November 21, 2008, at the Grace Baptist Christian School in Plymouth, Indiana. The cast was as follows:

DAVEY BRYANT. . . . . Kyle LaFaive

JOHN MASTERSON . . . . Zach West

BETH MASTERSON . . . . Katie Hickey

JD MASTERSON . . . . TJ Mechling

MEREDITH MASTERSON. . . . . Jessica Cleveland

TYLER MASTERSON. . . . . Ace Elliott

LEXI MASTERSON . . . . Madi Burns

PASTOR BRIAN MALONE. . . . . Logan Metzger

ERIN THOMPSON . . . . Heather Fishburn

KATIE THOMPSON . . . . Lena Gilbert

TARA THOMPSON . . . . Danielle LaFaive

MICK. . . . . Kaleb LaFaive

RILEY . . . . Phathai Mechling

CHARACTERS

DAVEY BRYANT – Age 12; bus kid; a deeper, goofy voice; acts tough but actually sensitive deep down; slovenly; awkward; no manners; secretly thrilled to have been invited to the Mastersons' for Thanksgiving; in awe of everything

JOHN MASTERSON – Age 35; bus driver for Faith Baptist Church bus ministry; outgoing, energetic, big-hearted, comical

BETH MASTERSON – Age 34; John's wife; helps John on his bus route each week; great cook; enjoys playing matchmaker, although she is usually not too good at it

JD MASTERSON – Age 12; ringleader of the Masterson kids; intelligent and highly creative; the idea mastermind

MEREDITH MASTERSON – Age 11; tomboy; competitive, argumentative; TYLER's protector

TYLER MASTERSON – Age 9; quiet, shy, easily embarrassed; Davey's favorite person to tease

LEXI MASTERSON – Age 7; plays up her role as baby of the family for all its worth; immense lung power; spunky; mischievous

PASTOR BRIAN MALONE – Age 28; Faith Baptist Church's new, single youth pastor; teaches junior church; all the little girls have crushes on him, including Meredith, Katie, and Tara

ERIN THOMPSON – Age 29; widowed mother of Katie and Tara; Beth tries to set her up with Pastor Brian

KATIE THOMPSON – Age 10; Meredith's friend; intelligent; bossy, especially toward her sister

TARA THOMPSON – Age 8; Katie's younger sister; greatly admires her sister and often imitates everything Katie says; a follower

MICK – JD's church friend; speaking part

RILEY – JD's church friend; speaking part; male or female

FAITH BAPTIST CHURCH MEMBERS – non-speaking parts

TIME

Modern-day; week of Thanksgiving

SETTING

Church foyer; Mastersons' barn; Mastersons' dining room

ACT I

Scene One

*(**SET**: Faith Baptist Church foyer; after the Sunday morning service the Sunday before Thanksgiving)*

*(Lights rise. **BETH** and **ERIN** stand at centerstage talking. Other church members also stand around talking to one another.)*

BETH. ...And so after we had spent nearly thirty minutes looking for it, I finally decided to forget about the timer and just baste the bird. I took the turkey out of the oven...and the thing was *ringing*! Lexi thought I meant put the timer *inside* the turkey!

*(**ERIN** and **BETH** laugh.)*

ERIN. And I thought *my* girls were the only ones who did crazy things like that!

BETH. Nope. You are definitely not alone there.

ERIN. Which reminds me...thank you so much for inviting us over for Thanksgiving. Are you sure it won't be any trouble having three extra people around?

BETH. Of course it's no trouble! John and I are looking forward to it. And I'm sure Meredith will be thrilled to have Katie and Tara over.

*(**MEREDITH** storms in, stage left, with **KATIE** and **TARA** trailing behind her.)*

MEREDITH. *(shouting indignantly)* Mom!

BETH. Well, what do you know? There's my little angel now.

*(turning to **MEREDITH**)*

Meredith, honey? What have I told you about yelling in church?

5

MEREDITH. Mom, do you know what Davey Bryant did in junior church this time?! He had this little plastic baggie full of crumbs and another one full of black ants and he –

BETH. All right, Meredith. That's enough tattling for one Sunday.

MEREDITH. But, Mo-om!

BETH. Guess what? I've got some good news for you!

MEREDITH. *(sulking)* Unless the good news is that Davey's moving to Madagascar, I'm not listening.

BETH. Noooooo. But Mrs. Thompson, Katie, and Tara are coming over for Thanksgiving.

KATIE. Really??

MEREDITH. They are?? All right!

(MEREDITH, KATIE, and TARA run off stage right, excited.)

ERIN. *(laughing)* Well, that was sure a sudden change of heart.

BETH. Yes. That's one of the great things about children – they're easily distractible. At least, I know Meredith is. …Now, what was I just about to tell you…?

(with feigned realization)

Oh! That's right. Where is my mind? Meredith must get that distractibility thing from me. I was *going* to tell you that John and I have also invited that new youth pastor, Pastor Brian, over for Thanksgiving dinner, too. I hoped you wouldn't mind.

(BETH shoots a sidelong glance at ERIN, trying to read her expression. ERIN's expression never changes.)

ERIN. Of course not.

BETH. It's just that he doesn't have anyone to spend Thanksgiving Day with either. Poor guy. It must be hard being single in a church of mostly marrieds.

ERIN. *(laughing)* Tell me about it.

BETH. Oh, Erin! I'm sorry. There I go again putting my foot in my mouth!

ERIN. Don't worry about it. Most people don't think of widows as single. I suppose we're a little bit better off. At least I have my girls. Sometimes I don't know what I'd do without them.

BETH. *(laughing)* Well, with *my* girls, sometimes I don't know what to do *with* them. I haven't told them yet that Pastor Brian's coming to dinner because I just know Meredith will go crazy. She has this huge crush on him. You should see her face when she gets out of his Sunday school class; she practically glows.

ERIN. I know. Katie and Tara are the same way. In fact, I hear he has that effect on most of the little girls in that class.

BETH. I suppose I should be grateful. I mean, she *could* have a crush on a singer or a movie star or a profes-sional athlete with green hair, six earrings, and a spike through his nose or something. At least the man she's looking up to is a man of God.

*(**JOHN** bounds up to **BETH** and **ERIN** energetically, stage right.)*

JOHN. Hey, Beth! Are you ready to go? The bus is waiting!

BETH. Oh, there you are, honey. I just invited Erin and the girls over for Thanksgiving dinner. I hope that's okay.

JOHN. Of course it is. You know my philosophy – the more the merrier!

BETH. *(whispering to **ERIN**)* That's why we ended up with so many kids.

*(**DAVEY** enters stage right, strutting across the stage toward stage left exit. He is holding one of **TYLER**'s dress shoes. **JOHN** grabs him by the shirt sleeve as he passes by the group of adults.)*

JOHN. *(good-naturedly)* Hey, there, Davey. Where do you think you're going? The bus is about to leave.

DAVEY. Oh. Hey, Mr. M. Hey, Mrs. M. I was just –

(**JD** *storms up behind them, stage right.* **TYLER** *follows*
JD, *hopping on one foot, his shoeless foot off the ground.*
JD *grabs the shoe from* **DAVEY** *and hands it to* **TYLER**,
who quickly puts it back on his foot in embarrassment.)

JD. *(fiercely) That is Tyler's* shoe, Davey!

BETH. JD! Manners, please!

DAVEY. *(innocently)* Tyler?…Oh! You must mean "Cinder-fella!"

(**MEREDITH** *and* **LEXI** *enter stage right.*)

MEREDITH. Mom! You should *see* the mess Davey made on the bus!

JD. Yeah. And then he stole Tyler's shoe and told him *he* had to clean it all up –

LEXI. *(loudly and shrilly)* And then he started running around singing, "Cinderfella, Cinderfella, day and night it's Cinderfella!"

(**BETH**, *looking slightly overwhelmed, cups her hands over* **LEXI***'s mouth.*)

BETH. Lexi! What have I told you?? Indoor voice, please!

(**BETH** *releases a pouting* **LEXI**. **DAVEY** *has been grinning and listening the entire time.* **JOHN** *turns to* **DAVEY** *good-naturedly.*)

JOHN. Well, young man, it seems as though you've got plenty of energy and some to spare. I guess our kids just aren't used to – Hey. Wait a minute. I've got an idea. Davey, do you have any plans for Thanksgiving?

JD. Uh-oh.

DAVEY. *(grinning broadly)* Nope.

JOHN. Well then…how would you like to come over to our house for Thanksgiving dinner on Thursday?

MASTERSON KIDS. What?!?

DAVEY. Really?? Oh boy! That'd be great!

JOHN. Well then, we'll ask your mom about it when we take you home today!

MASTERSON KIDS. WHAT?!?

DAVEY. Wow! A real Thanksgiving dinner! Thanks, Mr. M!

*(***DAVEY*** *runs offstage right.* **JOHN** *watches him run off, a smile on his face.)*

JOHN. Nice kid.

*(***JOHN*** *turns toward his own kids and finally notices them staring at him in shock.)*

What?

(The kids explode in a flurry of loud and fast complaints.)

JD. Dad...Are you *insane*???

MEREDITH. You just invited Davey "The Bully" Bryant over to our house! To our *house*!!

JD. I hope you're not expecting it to still be standing afterwards.

MEREDITH. Our house! Where we all *live*!

TYLER. *(whining; near tears)* I don't *wanna* have to eat my socks!

LEXI. *(shrilly; louder than all the rest combined)* He can't come over to our house! He's a boy! A mean, stinky, yucky – !

BETH. Lexi!! Indoor voice!

LEXI. *(even more loudly and shrilly)* But this *is* my indoor voice!!!

ERIN. *(to* **BETH***)* Uh...Beth? I'm sorry, but I'd better go find Katie and Tara.

BETH. *(apologetically)* Oh, Erin, I'm sorry. I hope we haven't scared you away from coming over for Thanksgiving.

ERIN. No. It's okay. We'll be there.

(The adults continue to "talk" silently while the kids confer.)

MEREDITH. *(under her breath)* You ought to be more worried about *Davey* scaring everyone away.

JD. *(to the kids)* All right, you guys. I think this calls for an emergency meeting of the Masterson kids. As soon as we get home!

MEREDITH. I'll see if Katie and Tara can come over, too. If they're going to be here for Thanksgiving dinner then *they'll* have to suffer through Davey too. They should come to the emergency meeting.

JD. *(grimly)* Sure thing. We're going to need all the help we can get.

(The adults finish "talking" and **ERIN** *exits stage right with a good-bye wave to* **BETH.** *Suddenly,* **BETH** *turns to* **JOHN,** *a confused look on her face.)*

BETH. John?

JOHN. *(playfully)* Yes, dear?

BETH. Didn't you say the bus was ready to go?

JOHN. Yep. Ready and running. All the kids are waiting.

BETH. *(slowly)* Well, if we're all in here…who's waiting with all those bus kids out there?

(There is a moment of silence as the **MASTERSONS** *stare at one another in horror.)*

(SOUND: Loud bus honking)

(The **MASTERSONS** *run offstage right.)*

(Lights fade.)

End of Scene

Scene Two

(SET: The Mastersons' barn; Sunday afternoon)

(Lights rise. The scene opens in confusion, all the kids talking, shouting, and whining at once, complaining about what will happen if Davey comes over. Suddenly, JD jumps up on a hay bale.)

JD. Okay, okay, everybody calm down! I call this meeting of the Masterson kids to order!

KATIE. The Masterson kids and guests.

JD. Right. The Masterson kids and guests.

(The kids all take up seats on nearby hay bales while JD remains standing.)

All right, guys –

KATIE. And girls.

JD. Right. Guys and girls …

(releasing a deep breath; dramatically)

We…have a serious problem here.

MEREDITH. *I'll* say!

JD. In just four days, our house will be invaded. By none other than –

LEXI. *(shrilly)* Martians?!?

TYLER. *(fearfully)* Martians??

JD. No!

TYLER. But you said we were going to be invaded!

JD. *(frustrated)* By Davey, you guys! Davey "The Bully" Bryant!

TYLER. Oh.

MEREDITH. I think I'd *rather* be invaded by Martians. At least then our house would be taken over by *intelligent* life.

JD. Okay, we're getting off the subject, guys.

KATIE. And girls.

JD. Right. Guys and girls. Okay. What my question to all of you is – what are we going to do about Davey?

(There is a moment of concerned silence.)

TYLER. *(softly)* If Davey's coming over here, I'm going to stay in my room and not come out the entire day.

MEREDITH. Tyler, you can't let Davey push you around like that! This is your Thanksgiving dinner, too!

(to the kids)

I say, we need to stand up to Davey!

(turning to **TYLER***)*

Besides…don't you want any turkey?

TYLER. No. I'm too chicken.

JD. Look, I think we all agree that Davey Bryant is a problem that has to be dealt with. But I don't think we need to stand *up* to Davey. I say, we need to get *rid* of Davey.

KATIE. Okay. But…how?

MEREDITH. Yeah. How?

JD. *(thoughtfully)* Well, the first step is talking Dad into letting Davey come over a little early on Thanksgiving Day to "help" with dinner.

(turning to **KATIE** *and* **TARA***)*

You two can come over early too.

KATIE. Thanks, but if Davey's going to be here, no thanks!

TARA. Yeah. No thanks!

JD. Oh, he won't be for long. Not if we can help it.

TARA. *(hushed)* What are you going to do?

JD. *(dramatically)* Come Thanksgiving Day, we're going to put on a little anti-bully campaign I like to call… "Davey Demolition Day."

MEREDITH. All right! He's gonna be sorry he ever set *foot* in *our* house!

LEXI. Yeah!

(The kids except for **TYLER** *start drawing together into a huddle.)*

TYLER. *(quietly speaking up)* Are you sure we can't just let the Martians have him?

(All the kids turn to look at TYLER. MEREDITH *sighs and puts an arm around* TYLER, *drawing him into the huddle as the lights fade.)*

End of Scene

Scene Three

(SET: Faith Baptist Church foyer; after the Wednesday evening service the day before Thanksgiving)

(Lights rise. **JD***, wearing a baseball cap, is standing at centerstage with* **MICK** *and* **RILEY**. **BETH** *is sitting stage right and upstage of the group of boys, looking over some papers.)*

MICK. *(to* **JD***)* Wow, man. I heard about Davey going over to your house for Thanksgiving tomorrow. Tough break.

RILEY. Yeah. I never thought I'd say this, but I am *so* glad I'm going to Grandma's for Thanksgiving.

JD. *(shrugging)* It's no big deal.

MICK. No big deal?? Aren't you worried he's going to smash all your stuff or something?

RILEY. Or burn down your barn?

MICK. Or blow up your house??

RILEY. *(slightly hysterical)* No, worse!…What if he eats all the pumpkin pie?!?

JD. *(smugly)* I don't think I'm going to need to worry about Davey Bryant. Because it just so happens that I've got a plan. A plan I like to call –

*(***DAVEY*** runs in, stage left.* **MICK** *and* **RILEY** *immediately look fearful.)*

DAVEY. *(tauntingly to* **JD***)* Hey! JP! Looks like I'm going to *your* house for Thanksgiving.

*(***DAVEY*** slings an arm around* **JD**. *The other guys inch away from him.)*

*(***JD*** gives* **DAVEY** *a dirty look and shoves his arm off of him.)*

JD. Yeah. Great. By the way, my name's not JP; it's JD.

DAVEY. JD? What's *that* stand for? Giant dimwit??

*(***DAVEY*** walks off stage left guffawing.* **JD**, **MICK**, *and* **RILEY** *exchange glances and then watch* **DAVEY** *leave.)*

JD. I don't like that kid.

RILEY. Who does?

(**DAVEY** *suddenly runs back in, stage left. He grabs* **JD** *'s hat.*)

DAVEY. Oh and by the way…thanks for the hat, PJ!

(**DAVEY** *runs offstage left.*)

JD. Okay. Now I *really* don't like that kid.

RILEY. *(patting* **JD** *'s shoulder)* My condolences.

MICK. Yeah. It's been nice knowing you, man.

(**RILEY** *and* **MICK** *exit stage right.* **JD** *heaves a sigh of frustration and marches off stage left.* **ERIN** *enters from stage left with* **KATIE** *and* **TARA** *in tow. She glances briefly at* **JD** *in concern as he passes them. Then* **ERIN** *crosses to* **BETH.** *)*

ERIN. Excuse me…Beth?

BETH. *(looking up)* Oh! Hi, Erin. Hi, girls. What's up?

KATIE. The sky.

TARA. Birds!!!

(**KATIE** *and* **TARA** *start laughing hysterically.*)

BETH. *(smiling good-naturedly)* I should have known better.

ERIN. Sorry. They're a little…wound up. …About dinner tomorrow …

BETH. *(disappointed)* Oh no! Please don't tell me you can't come!

ERIN. Oh! No, of course we're coming! In fact, I think the girls are really looking forward to it.

KATIE. Yeah. Thrilled.

(**ERIN** *gives* **KATIE** *a look and maneuvers* **KATIE** *behind her.*)

ERIN. I was just wondering if there is anything that I could bring.

BETH. Oh! Well, aren't you sweet? Perhaps –

(**PASTOR BRIAN** *steps in, stage left.*)

PASTOR BRIAN. Uh, Mrs. Masterson? Sorry to interrupt, but there's a bit of a...heated dispute going on back in the youth room between some of the kids. Something to do with JD's hat?

BETH. *(with a sigh)* Not again. I keep telling him not to wear that ratty old hat to church.

PASTOR BRIAN. Also, I was wondering...is there anything you need me to bring to dinner tomorrow?

BETH. *(delighted)* Oh! Well, what do you know about that? *Miss Thompson* here was just asking me the very same thing! She's also going to be joining us for dinner tomorrow.

PASTOR BRIAN. Oh, great. Well, you know what they say... the more, the merrier!

BETH. Yes, exactly! That's what my husband always says!

(BETH begins crossing toward stage left, stopping to grab KATIE and TARA by the arms as she passes.)

Well, why don't you two talk it out between yourselves, and whatever you decide to bring will be fine by me! I'll just take the girls with me and we'll go see if we can't figure out what all the fuss in the back is about, all right, girls?

KATIE. *(suspiciously)* You're not trying to get *rid* of us, are you?

TARA. *Are* you?

BETH. Get *rid* of you? Of course not! Whatever gave you that idea?

(to ERIN and PASTOR BRIAN)

We'll be back in a bit. Ten minutes, fifteen, maybe...an hour. Take your time!

(BETH hustles KATIE and TARA offstage left. PASTOR BRIAN and ERIN look at one another shyly. There is a brief pause.)

PASTOR BRIAN. Uh...so...what are your feelings on pumpkin pie?

ERIN. Favorable. Especially when there's whipped topping involved.

(PASTOR BRIAN *and* ERIN, *still "talking" silently, exit stage right. After a few moments,* BETH *peers in at them, stage left. She smiles happily.* JOHN, *walking up behind her, startles her out of her reverie.*)

JOHN. What are you doing?

BETH. Oh! John! You scared me!

JOHN. Okay, Beth, what's going on?

BETH. *(innocently)* Nothing. I'm just...doing my Thanksgiving good deed.

JOHN. *(folding his arms, skeptically)* Uh-huh. You wouldn't happen to be meddling in anyone's personal affairs, now would you?

BETH. Meddling? No, of course not! I'm just... *(in a rush)* trying to get Erin and Pastor Brian together.

JOHN. Oh, no. Not again!

BETH. *(wounded)* What do you mean, "Oh, no. Not again!"? I've never tried to get them together before!

JOHN. You're right. You *haven't* tried to get them together before. And that's probably the only reason they're still speaking to one another.

BETH. John! That is so unfair.

JOHN. Unfair?? Don't tell me you don't remember all of your other church member matches gone awry.

BETH. Well...they didn't *all* go badly. What about George Schumann and Wilma Applegate? *They're* still great friends.

JOHN. Beth...he ran over her cat...on the first date! She wouldn't talk to him for nearly a month! And that was only after he went out and bought her a new Himalayan. Do you have any idea how *expensive* those cats are??

BETH. Well, what's one dead cat? She had fourteen others. Besides, "The course of true love never did run smoothly."

JOHN. Yes, I suppose that explains the Anita-and-Samuel fiasco. And Mr. Williamson and our *former* organist Miss Richards. Oh, and don't forget about –

BETH. Okay, okay. I get the picture.

JOHN. Face it, sweetheart. You're good at a lot of things, but...matchmaking is just *not* one of them.

BETH. Humph.

JOHN. Now, if we're going to have Pastor Brian and Miss Thompson over for Thanksgiving, I want you to *promise* me that you're not going to interfere in their personal lives, all right?...All right?

BETH. *(heaving a huge, disappointed sigh)* Fine. I guess I'll just leave them alone and let them stay miserable.

JOHN. *(patting **BETH** on the arm)* That's a good girl. You're doing the right thing.

*(**JOHN** peers past **BETH** toward stage right exit.)*

(calling offstage)

Lexi?! Honey, that's not our car! Now put down that antenna this instant!

*(**JOHN** hurries off stage right.)*

BETH. Well...*I* may not be allowed to meddle, but that doesn't mean the two of them can't figure out on their own how perfect they are for each other. And if it just so happens to be while they're at our house enjoying a lovely Thanksgiving dinner, well...so be it!

*(**BETH** cheerfully exits stage left.)*

(Lights fade.)

End of Scene

ACT II

Scene One

(SET: The Mastersons' dining room; Thursday morning)

(Lights rise slowly. There is a long moment of peaceful silence, and then JOHN *suddenly bursts onto the scene from stage right and quickly crosses to centerstage.)*

JOHN. *(calling off stage left)* Goooooooood morning, everyone! Gobble, gobble! It's Thanksgiving Day! Get down here, you sleepyheads!

*(*LEXI *bursts in from stage left, followed by a somber* TYLER, *a grouchy* MEREDITH, *and a sleepy* JD.*)*

LEXI. Hi, Dad! Happy Thanks –

*(*LEXI *comes to a sudden stop as she catches sight of* JOHN.*)*

Aw, man! You're not wearing the turkey costume!

MEREDITH. Great. Then I've got something to be thankful about. Now can I go back to bed?

JOHN. Oh, come on now, Meredith. You don't *really* want to waste this beautiful Thanksgiving Day in *bed*, do you?

MEREDITH. Is that a rhetorical question?

JOHN. Now…I'm looking for volunteers! I need one person to come with me to go get Davey. The rest of you will stay behind to help your mother with kitchen duty. So…which one of you lucky little giblets wants to ride with me over to Jefferson Park?

*(*JD, MEREDITH, *and* LEXI *look at one another and then turn to look at* TYLER.*)*

TYLER. What??? Me?!?!

JD. *(whispering)* You know the plan.

TYLER. *(whimpering)* But…but…but!…Do I have to??

JD. *(confidently to* **JOHN***)* Tyler'll go, Dad.

JOHN. Great! Then let's get a move-on, little man. Hurry on upstairs and get dressed!

(With a pained sigh, **TYLER** *trudges offstage left.* **JOHN** *rubs his hands together eagerly as* **JD** *and* **MEREDITH** *flop down into chairs.)*

Okay! And while we're waiting, I think I'll pop into the kitchen and take a look-see at that turkey!

*(***JOHN*** *exits stage left. As soon as he leaves,* **LEXI** *jumps up and begins to skip around the room singing "Turkey in the Straw," quietly at first, but growing louder and louder with each repetition. At first,* **JD** *and* **MEREDITH** *talk over her.)*

MEREDITH. Have you ever noticed how much goofier Dad seems to get on holidays?

JD. Yeah. It is kinda strange, isn't it? This morning he came into my room and woke me up with a wild turkey call.

MEREDITH. That's funny. I thought Mom hid that from him last year.

JD. She did. I guess he must have found it.

MEREDITH. Well, it couldn't have been *too* hard. Mom's only got one hiding place.

JD & MEREDITH. Under the bed.

JD. Which, if you think about it, with all that other stuff she's got under there, it really does make a pretty good hiding spot. In fact, I bet –

*(***JD*** *suddenly whirls to face* **LEXI***.)*

Lexi! For crying out loud!!

JD & MEREDITH. *(shouting; irritated)* Indoor voice!!

*(***LEXI*** *stops skipping and turns to face them, screwing up her face.)*

LEXI. *(even more loudly)* YOU MEAN *THIS* ONE?!?

(BETH enters from stage left, JOHN trailing behind her, a pleading puppy dog expression on his face.)

BETH. No, John! I mean it. We are *not* dragging out that turkey costume this year. I want this to be a *nice* dinner for Erin and Pastor Brian and the girls.

MEREDITH. *(suddenly perking up)* Pastor *Brian* is coming for dinner??

JD. *(wryly)* And don't forget about Davey. He's coming over too.

BETH. Right. And Davey too. I just want it to be a nice, *normal* Thanksgiving dinner.

JD. *(under his breath)* You should have thought about that before you invited *Davey* over.

BETH. *(to JOHN)* John, we've talked about this.

JOHN. *(glumly)* All right, all right, no turkey costume.

(after a moment's thought, eagerly)

How about if I dress up like a pilgrim?

(BETH gives JOHN a look.)

Fine. But I'll have you know it's not much of a Thanksgiving if neither turkey nor pilgrims are present.

BETH. I'm sure we'll be able to make do just fine without them.

(TYLER enters from stage left, glumly, now dressed for the day.)

JOHN. There you are, sport! Ready to go?

TYLER. *(heaving a sigh)* I guess.

(Head down, like a man condemned to the gallows, TYLER trudges to downstage right exit.)

(over his shoulder)

If I'm not back in an hour, you'll know where to find my remains.

(TYLER exits downstage right. JOHN watches him leave, shaking his head and smiling.)

JOHN. We'll be back in a little bit.

 *(**JOHN** exits downstage right. **BETH** turns to **JD**, **MEREDITH**, and **LEXI**.)*

BETH. Well, kids, it looks like we've got about fifteen minutes to straighten this place up before company arrives.

JD. "Dum da dum dum."

LEXI. Davey Bryant's not company, Mom. He's just a big bully! A big, mean, stinky, yucky –

BETH. *(sternly)* Kids, Davey is our guest today, and I want you to be nice to him. Do I make myself clear?

 (The kids exchange glances.)

JD. Yeah. Okay, Mom.

BETH. Good. All right then. You three get things ready in here and I'll go check on that turkey.

 *(**BETH** exits stage left.)*

JD. Oh, we'll get things ready in here, won't we?

 *(**JD** turns to **MEREDITH**, who is still staring off into space dreamily.)*

 Uh, hello?…Meredith?

MEREDITH. Huh?…Oh, yeah! Ready!

 *(**MEREDITH** suddenly looks down at her pajamas.)*

 Yikes! I'm not ready at all! I've got to get dressed before Pastor Brian gets here!

JD. Meredith! That's not what I –

 *(**MEREDITH** races offstage left.)*

 Oh brother.

 *(turning to **LEXI**)*

 Well, it looks like it's just you and me, Short Stuff. Okay. Time to put Plan A into action.

LEXI. Plan A?

JD. Yep. Plan A…The Arrival.

 *(**JD** holds up a long piece of twine and smiles evilly.)*

LEXI. Ohhhhhhhh!

(LEXI *smiles, nods, and follows* JD *as he crosses to stage right.*)

Hey, JD? I just have one question.

(JD *stops walking and turns to* LEXI.)

JD. Yeah?

LEXI. What's a "giblet"?

(*Lights fade.*)

End of Scene

Scene Two

(SET: The Mastersons' dining room; Thursday morning)

(Lights rise. **BETH** *is setting the dining room table at centerstage.)*

*(***MEREDITH*** *enters, stage left, and watches* **BETH** *quietly.* **MEREDITH** *is wearing a frilly Sunday dress.* **BETH** *does not notice her at first. After a few moments of silence,* **MEREDITH** *speaks up.)*

MEREDITH. Hey, Mom.

*(***BETH*** *jumps.)*

BETH. *(glancing over her shoulder)* Oh! Honey! I didn't hear you come in. You startled me!

*(***BETH*** *places the last plate and then turns and gives her full attention to* **MEREDITH.***)*

Why, Meredith! Don't you look nice!

MEREDITH. *(embarrassed)* Thanks.

BETH. Is that the dress your Aunt Macey sent? Turn around. Let me see it.

(Eyes on the ground, **MEREDITH** *does a quick, self-conscious spin.)*

(smiling knowingly)

I don't think I've ever seen you voluntarily put on a dress! Mind if I ask what's the occasion?

MEREDITH. *(mumbling)* No reason. I just felt like it, that's all.

BETH. Well, you look very nice, sweetheart.

*(***BETH*** *picks up a stack of silverware from the table and begins laying down the place settings.* **MEREDITH** *follows behind her, watching.)*

MEREDITH. Yeah. Thanks….Hey, Mom?

BETH. *(smiling)* Hey, yeah?

MEREDITH. Uh…about what you said earlier …

BETH. I really meant it, honey! You look very nice.

MEREDITH. No. I mean about…um…about Pastor Brian. Is he really coming to dinner today?

BETH. Yes, sweetie, he is. Why?

MEREDITH. Just wondering.

(**BETH** *resumes setting the table and* **MEREDITH** *continues following her until* **MEREDITH** *suddenly bursts out in a rush.*)

Mom-can-I-sit-next-to-him-at-dinner?…Please???

BETH. What? Sit next to who?…Pastor Brian?! Oh, honey, I don't think –

(SOUND: Door bell)

(looking at her watch)

That must be Erin and the girls.

(**BETH** *sets down the silverware.*)

MEREDITH. Please, Mom????

BETH. Meredith, I've already laid out place cards, see? I'm sorry, honey. Maybe next time.

(**BETH** *crosses to the door while* **MEREDITH** *looks down at the table and sulks.* **BETH** *"opens" the door and* **ERIN**, **KATIE**, *and* **TARA** *enter downstage right.* **ERIN** *is carrying two pumpkin pies.*)

Hello! Happy Thanksgiving!

ERIN. Happy Thanksgiving!

TARA. *(eagerly)* We brought pumpkin pie!

ERIN. Yes. We brought pumpkin pie. I hope that's okay.

BETH. Of course! We *love* pumpkin pie! Here. Let me help you with that. Why don't we take them into the kitchen?

(**BETH** *and* **ERIN** *exit stage left while* **KATIE** *and* **TARA** *cross to* **MEREDITH**, *who is still standing by the table, looking down at the place cards.*)

KATIE. *(to* **MEREDITH**, *eagerly)* So…how's the anti-Davey campaign going?

TARA. Yeah! Did you anti-Davey yet?

MEREDITH. *(shrugging indifferently)* It's going okay, I guess. He's not here yet.

*(As **MEREDITH** talks, she reaches out and switches her place card with **ERIN**'s. **KATIE** and **TARA** watch her curiously.)*

KATIE. What are you doing?

MEREDITH. Pastor Brian's coming over for Thanksgiving dinner too.

KATIE. Pastor Brian?? Really?? He is?!?

TARA. Oh boy! I *love* Pastor Brian!

KATIE. I know! This is so great!!

*(noticing **MEREDITH**'s glum expression)*

Hey, wait a minute. You're in love with Pastor Brian, too. Why aren't you more excited?

MEREDITH. *(with a sigh)* Well, it seems as though we've got a bit of a problem.

TARA. Yeah. His name's Davey Bryant!

MEREDITH. No, I mean another bit of a problem. …. I think my mom wants your mom to marry Pastor Brian.

KATIE. What?! No! She can't! *I'm* going to marry him!… When I grow up, that is.

TARA. Yeah! Me too!

MEREDITH. Me three. But what are we going to do? If Pastor Brian comes over here and eats your mom's pie, he might fall in love with her.

TARA. *(worriedly)* Yeah. He just might. Mom's pie *is* pretty good.

KATIE. Well…what can we *do* about it??

TARA. Hide the pie?

MEREDITH. *(thoughtfully)* No…I think I've got a better idea. What if the three of us put on our *own* campaign?…An anti-love campaign!

KATIE. An anti-love campaign? But…but what about the anti-Davey campaign? Isn't JD going to need our help?

MEREDITH. Nah. JD and Tyler and Lexi can handle it. *We* need to focus on what's *really* important – keeping Pastor Brian and your mom apart.

KATIE. Right.

TARA. Right!

MEREDITH. Okay then. Let the anti-love campaign begin!

(Lights fade.)

End of Scene

Scene Three

(SET: The Mastersons' dining room; Thursday noon)

(Lights rise. **JD**, **MEREDITH**, **KATIE**, *and* **TARA** *are hanging around the dining room table, talking.* **LEXI** *is once again running around playing by herself.)*

(SOUND: A sudden crash off stage right)

MEREDITH. What was *that*??

DAVEY. *(offstage right) (sing-songy)* I'm heeeeeeeeeeeeeerrrrrre!

JD. *(hissing under his breath)* Quick! That's him! Everyone, assume your positions!

TARA. What?

(to **KATIE***; confused)*

Consume your physicians?!

KATIE. *(impatiently)* Tara!! *This* way!

*(***KATIE*** grabs* **TARA** *and pulls her beneath the table while* **JD** *pulls a chair toward downstage right and quickly sits. He leans back as though relaxing.* **DAVEY** *bounds in from downstage right.)*

DAVEY. Hey, JR! How's it goin'? Where's the grub? I'm starvin – Whoa!!

(After quickly messing up **JD***'s hair,* **DAVEY** *bounds past* **JD***'s chair – and promptly trips and falls on his face over the twine the kids have pulled taut. The kids hide their snickers behind their hands.)*

JD. Wow. Davey…I had no idea you were so…graceful.

MEREDITH. Yeah. Have a nice trip? See you next fall.

*(***BETH*** enters, stage left, carrying a stack of napkins, a worried look on her face, seemingly oblivious to the fact that* **DAVEY** *is facedown on the floor. The kids sit and stand up a little straighter and exchange nervous glances.)*

DAVEY. *(still flat on the floor)* Hey, Mrs. M. Cool rug.

BETH. Why, thank you, Davey.

(DAVEY gets to his feet and looks around the room in satisfaction. The kids look at one another in disappointment. BETH sets the stack of napkins on the table as JOHN enters from downstage right. He talks to her as he crosses toward the table.)

JOHN. *(to BETH)* Beth! There you are! Okay. About the costume…How about we make a deal?

BETH. No.

(BETH exits stage left, JOHN following right behind her, wheedling.)

JOHN. Aw, come on, dear. How many times a year does a man get the opportunity to dress up like a giant turkey??

(JOHN exits stage left.)

DAVEY. *(looking around)* Yep. This is a pretty cool house, RJ.

JD. My name is JD!

(TYLER enters from downstage right. His button-down shirt is pulled up over his head [he is wearing a T-shirt under his dress shirt], forcing his arms to stick straight up in the air and covering his head.

MEREDITH. Tyler! What happened to you??

(At the sound of his name, TYLER lowers his arms so that he can peer out at the audience through the head hole of the shirt. MEREDITH rushes to help peel TYLER's shirt back down.)

DAVEY. Aw, we were just playing a little game, weren't we, Typo? And he lost.

(turning to the others)

So. When do we eat?? I'm starving!

JD. Well, that's too bad. Because we can't eat yet. Not until the food's all ready.

DAVEY. Oh. Okay. Then I'll help.

(DAVEY heads toward stage left. The kids jump in front of him to block his way.)

JD, MEREDITH, & KATIE. NO!!!

(DAVEY stops and gives them a curious look.)

JD. *(thinking on his feet)* I mean, wait a minute. Not in there. What we actually need is...

KATIE. Someone to go get us the Thanksgiving turkey!

DAVEY. The turkey? You mean, like, at the supermarket??

MEREDITH. No...In the woods!

DAVEY. In the woods?

KATIE. *(skeptically)* In the woods?!?

JD. Yeah. In the woods. It's a Masterson family tradition. We do it every year.

DAVEY. Really? And what am I supposed to catch this turkey with?

JD. Uh ...

(JD looks around hastily and picks up a slingshot from the table.)

(exultantly)

With this!

MEREDITH. Hey! That's *my* slingshot!

JD. *(whispering tightly)* Well, *you* were the one who came up with the turkey in the woods!

(MEREDITH crosses her arms and sulks. JD hands the slingshot to DAVEY.)

Here you go!

DAVEY. If this *is* a Masterson family tradition...then why haven't you done it already?

JD. Uh, because we were...waiting for you!

MEREDITH. Yeah. We know how much you like to slingshot stuff.

LEXI. And throw stuff.

JD. And steal stuff.

TYLER. And scare stuff…I mean, people. …I mean…me.

DAVEY. *(thoughtfully)* Yeah. You're right. I do.

KATIE. Besides, turkeys usually only come out in the afternoon. They like to sleep late.

> *(All the kids, including DAVEY, turn to look at KATIE in disbelief.)*

> *(whispering to JD)*

> What?? You said, be creative!

JD. *Anyways…*

> *(turning to DAVEY)*

> Are you going to get the turkey or not?

DAVEY. Yeah. Alright. I'll get your turkey for you, AJ –

MEREDITH. Great! See you!

DAVEY. But one of you is coming with me.

> *(The kids look at one another for a long moment. Then they all turn to look at TYLER.)*

TYLER. Me?!?

> *(The kids continue to stare at TYLER.)*

> *(with a dejected sigh)*

> All right. Fine. I'll go. But this is *so* not fair.

> *(DAVEY slings his arm around TYLER's shoulder as they move toward the upstage center exit.)*

DAVEY. Hey, Typo! I've got a great idea. Let's play another game! This time, I can be the hunter, and you can be the turkey!

> *(TYLER groans as TYLER and DAVEY exit. MEREDITH turns to JD nervously.)*

MEREDITH. Tyler's going to be okay, isn't he?

JD. Don't worry. It's just a plastic slingshot. I'm sure Davey can't do too much damage with it.

> *(SOUND: A shouted "Yow!" offstage)*

MEREDITH. That's what *you* think!

JD. All right, you guys. Time for Plan B…The Bowl!

*(**JD**, **LEXI**, **KATIE**, **TARA**, and **MEREDITH** move toward stage left exit. **JD** and **LEXI** exit.)*

(SOUND: Doorbell)

*(At the sound of the doorbell, **MEREDITH** grabs **KATIE** and **TARA** and pulls them back into the dining room.)*

MEREDITH. Wait a minute! Listen! I think that's him!…I think he's here!!

KATIE. Who's here?

MEREDITH. *You* know! Pastor Brian!!

(SOUND: Doorbell)

(The girls squeal excitedly.)

BETH. *(offstage)* Erin? Do you think you could do me a favor and answer the door?

ERIN. *(offstage)* Sure thing.

MEREDITH. Quick! Hide!

*(The girls duck underneath the table. Just as **ERIN** enters, stage left, **PASTOR BRIAN** pokes his head in through the downstage right "door.")*

PASTOR BRIAN. Hello? Anybody home?

ERIN. Pastor Brian! Hello!

*(**PASTOR BRIAN** steps into the dining room.)*

PASTOR BRIAN. Happy Thanksgiving!

ERIN. Yes. Happy Thanksgiving.

*(**PASTOR BRIAN** and **ERIN** smile awkwardly at one another for a long moment. Finally, **PASTOR BRIAN** holds up a plastic grocery bag.)*

PASTOR BRIAN. I…brought Cool Whip.

ERIN. Oh. Cool Whip. Great!

(There is another long pause.)

PASTOR BRIAN. *(unsure)* For the pumpkin pie?

ERIN. *(laughing lightly)* Yes. For the pumpkin pie. I know. You didn't think I eat Cool Whip right out of the container, did you?

PASTOR BRIAN. *(embarrassed)* No. No, of course not.

ERIN. Well, actually…sometimes I do.

PASTOR BRIAN. *(relieved)* Really? So do I! I mean, when you're out of ice cream, Cool Whip makes a great second choice.

ERIN. Especially since they have the fat-free kind.

PASTOR BRIAN. Yeah. Well, it's not like *you* need it.

(PASTOR BRIAN *and* ERIN *smile at one another and lapse into a self-conscious but pleasant silence.* MEREDITH *suddenly pops out of hiding, placing herself between* PASTOR BRIAN *and* ERIN.)

MEREDITH. *(loudly)* Hi, Pastor Brian! What's in the bag?

(MEREDITH *grabs the bag from him as* KATIE *and* TARA *pop out of hiding beside* ERIN.)

Cool Whip? You brought Cool Whip?! Great! Cool Whip is my absolutely most favoritest thing in the entire world!

(dreamily; turning to KATIE *and* TARA)

Look, you guys! Pastor Brian brought Cool Whip!

(KATIE *grabs one of* ERIN*'s hands.*)

KATIE. *(whining)* Mom! I want some pumpkin pie!

TARA. *(grabbing* ERIN*'s other hand)* Yeah. Me too!

ERIN. Honey, those pies are for dessert. We have to wait until –

KATIE. But I want pumpkin pie right NOW!

TARA. Me too!!

(KATIE *and* TARA *drag* ERIN *toward stage left exit.*)

ERIN. *(to* PASTOR BRIAN, *with a laugh)* Looks like I'd better get back to work.

PASTOR BRIAN. Yeah, well, the sooner dinner's ready, the sooner we get to have dessert, right?

ERIN. *(with a laugh)* Right. And Cool Whip.

PASTOR BRIAN. And Cool Whip.

> *(**KATIE** and **TARA** drag **ERIN** off stage left. There is a moment of silence. **MEREDITH**, hugging the Cool Whip to her chest, stares up at **PASTOR BRIAN** dreamily. **PASTOR BRIAN** looks around uncomfortably and after a long moment clears his throat.)*

PASTOR BRIAN. Maybe I should…uh…go put that Cool Whip in the refrigerator.

MEREDITH. Oh! That's okay, Pastor Brian. I can do it!

> *(**MEREDITH** runs off stage left. **PASTOR BRIAN** lets out a relieved breath. He looks around at the dining room table. Suddenly, he does a double take as he notices the place cards beside each setting. He hurriedly exchanges **MEREDITH**'s place card with **ERIN**'s. Smiling, he exits, stage left.)*

> *(Lights fade.)*

End of Scene

ACT III

Scene One

(SET: The Mastersons' dining room; Thursday afternoon)

(Lights rise. All the kids except **TYLER** *and* **DAVEY** *are huddled in the center of the dining room.)*

JD. Okay. Plan B is ready for action. All we need to do is lure Davey into the kitchen and that big bowl of mashed potatoes will fall right onto his head!

MEREDITH. Where are Mom and Dad?

JD. Lexi? The spy report, please.

*(**LEXI** stands at attention and salutes.)*

KATIE. You made *Lexi* the spy? Kind of a leap of faith, don't you think?

TARA. Yeah. She *is* a little loud.

MEREDITH. A little???

LEXI. *(loudly and self-importantly)* Ahem. Dad went to the store. To get more milk...I think. And Mom's upstairs hiding his turkey costume under the bed.

(turning to **MEREDITH**)

So there!

*(**LEXI** sticks out her tongue at* **MEREDITH***.)*

JD. Okay. So this is our window of opportunity. Let's go find Davey!

*(**JD**, **MEREDITH**, **KATIE**, **TARA**, and **LEXI** exit upstage center. A few moments later, **JOHN** enters from downstage right, looking around the dining room, puzzled. He pats his pockets as he walks.)*

JOHN. *(slowly; to himself)* Hmmm…now where in the world did I put my wallet?…I know! Maybe it's in the kitchen.

(JOHN exits, stage left.)

(SOUND: Loud crash and JOHN's shout)

(All the kids, including TYLER and DAVEY, come running in upstage center.)

MEREDITH. What was *that*?!?

JD. I don't know, but it sounded like –

JOHN. *(offstage) (bellowing)* KIDS!!!!!

JD. *(fearful squeak)* – Dad.

DAVEY. All right! There's *always* something exciting going on here!

(DAVEY races off, stage left.)

DAVEY. *(offstage)* Hey, Mr. M!…Why are you all covered in mashed potatoes? Is it time to eat??

JD. *(to LEXI)* I thought you said Dad went to the store???

KATIE. Told you it was a leap of faith.

JOHN. *(offstage)* JD!!! Would you come here for a minute, please!!!

(JD turns nervously to the other kids.)

JD. Oh boy. Uh…okay. Just in case I don't happen to come back…*ever*…Meredith, you're in charge. It's time for Plan C.

MEREDITH. Plan C. Got it.

JOHN. *(offstage)* JD!!!!!!!!

(JD slinks offstage left just as DAVEY reenters from stage left, licking his fingers.)

DAVEY. Mmmmmm-mmmh! These are some of the best mashed potatoes I've ever tasted! What kinda box does your mom use?

LEXI. Box? Potatoes don't come from a box!

DAVEY. Sure they do. They look like little paper flakes and then you mix them up with milk. But if you don't have milk, you can use water. That's what we always use.

(The girls exchange disgusted looks.)

KATIE. Ew.

TARA. Double ew.

LEXI. We don't eat box potatoes. We only eat *real* potatoes. The kind you peel.

DAVEY. Wow! Well then, you sure are lucky!

(The girls and TYLER exchange somewhat guilty looks. DAVEY turns to TYLER, a mischievous gleam in his eye.)

Well...guess we better get back to our turkey hunt, eh, Typo?

TYLER. Uh.....

(TYLER turns pleading eyes on MEREDITH.)

MEREDITH. Uh...actually, Davey, I was wondering if you could do me a favor.

DAVEY. A favor?

MEREDITH. Yeah. Do you think you could...uh...feed Sparky for me?

DAVEY. Sparky? Who's Sparky?

LEXI. Yeah. Who's Sparky?

MEREDITH. *You* know. Sparky. Our dog Sparky?

DAVEY. *(excitedly)* A dog? You have a dog? Really? Cool! What kind of dog is he?

MEREDITH. He's a....a...

KATIE. *(simultaneously)* A Schnauzer!

LEXI. *(simultaneously)* A Dalmatian!

DAVEY. Huh?

MEREDITH. They mean, he's a schnauzer with *spots*, like a Dalmatian!

DAVEY. Oh. ...He sounds ugly.

LEXI. *(indignantly)* He's not ugly! He's our dog!

DAVEY. Okay. Whatever. So where is he?

MEREDITH. He's...in the barn. So is his dog food. You may have to look around a little for him; he really likes to hide in the hay.

DAVEY. Okay. Sounds easy enough. You coming, Typo?

(**TYLER** *shakes his head fervently.* **DAVEY** *shrugs.*)

Suit yourself.

(**DAVEY** *moves toward upstage center exit.*)

Here, puppy, puppy, puppy!

(**DAVEY** *exits upstage center.*)

LEXI. *(to* **MEREDITH,** *excitedly)* We got a dog?? I didn't know we got a dog!!

MEREDITH. *(rolling her eyes)* We *didn't*, Lexi. I was just trying to get Davey out of the house, remember?

LEXI. Oh.… Phooey. I want a dog!

MEREDITH. Okay, you guys. You heard what JD said. It's time for Plan C…Plan Canine!

(*The kids start grabbing* **DAVEY**'s *place setting from the table.*)

(*Lights fade.*)

End of Scene

Scene Two

(SET: The Mastersons' dining room; Thursday afternoon)

(Lights rise. Everyone except DAVEY and JOHN is in the dining room. On the stage right side of the table, BETH stands between PASTOR BRIAN and ERIN, encouraging them to talk. JD is sitting in a chair by himself at downstage left, sulking. MEREDITH, KATIE, and TARA stand huddled together at upstage center, occasionally sneaking worried glances at PASTOR BRIAN and ERIN. TYLER is looking out upstage center exit nervously and LEXI is running around playing a game by herself. The table is now fully decorated and set for Thanksgiving dinner, and all the food except for the turkey is on the table.)

BETH. *(to PASTOR BRIAN)* ...and did you know that it was Miss Thompson here who organized that entire food drive herself?

PASTOR BRIAN. Wow! That's pretty impressive!

ERIN. Oh, it wasn't really that –

BETH. *I'll* say it is! The church ended up collecting something like, what was it, Erin? Fifteen hundred pounds of canned goods??

ERIN. Something like that.

PASTOR BRIAN. Wow. That's a lot of baked beans!

ERIN. *(laughing)* And carrots and green beans and creamed corn!

BETH. Speaking of which, I don't know about anyone else, but *I'm* getting hungry.

(aloud to everyone present)

Why don't we all take a seat and I'll see if I can't find John?

(The kids cross to the dining room table and take a seat. PASTOR BRIAN gallantly pulls a chair out for ERIN.)

PASTOR BRIAN. Miss Thompson.

ERIN. Why, thank you!

(ERIN sits, PASTOR BRIAN smiling down at her. MEREDITH watches them, horrified. Suddenly, she begins coughing frantically as though she's choking.)

BETH. Meredith! What's the matter?

KATIE. I think she's choking!

TARA. She's choking!!!

(PASTOR BRIAN, ERIN, KATIE, TARA, and BETH jump up from their seats. Her goal accomplished, MEREDITH's "choking" dies down. She delicately sits, sighs happily, and smiles to herself. Everyone cautiously resumes sitting, staring at MEREDITH uncertainly.)

ERIN. Meredith…Are you okay?

MEREDITH. *(under her breath)* I was fine until you stole my seat.

ERIN. I'm sorry?

MEREDITH. *(more loudly)* Uh, I said, I'm fine. And…aren't you sweet?

BETH. What in the world was *that* all about?

MEREDITH. Sorry, Mom. Must have…been a chicken bone.

BETH. Meredith, honey…we're having turkey.

MEREDITH. Oh. I meant, a turkey bone.

BETH. And your father hasn't even carved the turkey yet.

MEREDITH. Oh.

(MEREDITH shoots a furtive glance over at PASTOR BRIAN and ERIN. Everyone resumes their seats as JOHN enters stage left, carrying a large turkey on a platter and wearing his turkey costume.)

JOHN. *(jovially)* Did somebody say "turkey"?

BETH. *(dropping her head into her hands)* Oh no.

LEXI. Yay! Daddy!!!

(JOHN crosses to the table and sets the platter down. Both PASTOR BRIAN and ERIN carefully study the turkey on the platter to avoid looking at JOHN.)

PASTOR BRIAN. *(trying not to laugh)* My, that…um…sure is one nice-looking bird.

MASHED POTATOES AND DAVEY

ERIN. Yes. It...has such a nice, golden-brown color.

JOHN. Why, thank you. The one my wife cooked is not so bad-looking either.

BETH. *(her head still in her hands)* I've got to find a new hiding spot.

JOHN. So...are we ready to pray and dig in?

(JD clears his throat and gives MEREDITH a pointed look.)

MEREDITH. Oh! Right! Uh...Wait a minute, Dad. Where's Davey?

(SOUND: Door slamming)

(DAVEY enters upstage center.)

DAVEY. Hey, uh, guys? I hate to be the one with the bad news, but I think your dog ran away.

BETH. Dog? What dog?

MEREDITH. *(hurriedly)* Dog? What are you talking about? We don't have a dog.

DAVEY. But you said –

JD. Hurry up and sit down, Davey. The food's getting cold.

DAVEY. Food! All right!

(DAVEY runs over to the table. He suddenly stops short when he notices all the places at the table are filled. He looks around the room slowly, stopping when he sees his place setting sitting on the floor of downstage left. His plate has been replaced with a dog bowl.)

MEREDITH. *(giggling)* Oh. I guess we do have a dog!

(For a moment, DAVEY looks hurt as the other kids laugh.)

JOHN. *(shocked)* Kids!

(The kids stop laughing and guiltily turn to look at JOHN. Seeing him in his turkey costume, they stifle giggles.)

BETH. *(to JOHN, quietly)* Kind of difficult to be the voice of authority dressed as a turkey, wouldn't you agree, honey?

JOHN. *(to* BETH*)* You're right. As soon as we're done here, I'll break out the Pilgrim costume.

(turning back to the kids)

Kids! This kind of behavior is unacceptable! We've invited Davey into our *home*, and –

(DAVEY *takes a seat in downstage left corner, stretching his legs out in front of him and leaning back on his hands comfortably.)*

DAVEY. Hey, it's okay, Mr. M. Really. I'm used to this. My family and I never eat around the table anyway. Usually, we don't eat meals together at all.

(Once again, the kids look at one another guiltily.)

TYLER. *(softly)* What about on Christmas?

DAVEY. *(sarcastically)* Christmas? What's that?

TARA. What about on your birthday?

DAVEY. My birthday? Let's see…last year, Mom was working.

JD. And where was your dad?

DAVEY. Prison.

BETH. *(quietly)* What is your family doing today, Davey?

DAVEY. Today? You mean, for Thanksgiving? Nothing. I mean, to us, it's just another day. That's why *I'm* so thankful I get to eat *here* this year. Turkey and stuffin' and peas and corn and pie and real potatoes that don't come from a box! Yum!

(There is a moment of silence. DAVEY *jumps to his feet with the dog bowl and crosses to the food on the table.)*

DAVEY. Do you mind if I…?

JOHN. Not at all. You go ahead and help yourself, young man. Here. Take my plate.

DAVEY. Thanks!

*(*DAVEY *sets the dog bowl on the table, takes* JOHN*'s plate, and begins filling the plate with food while the kids just look solemnly at one another. The adults watch the kids.)*

JD. Uh, Dad? May I...may I be excused? I need to, um, go blow my nose.

JOHN. *(knowingly)* Of course, son.

(*JD stands up and moves toward upstage center exit, stopping briefly to kick MEREDITH's chair.*)

MEREDITH. Oh. Right. Mom, may I be excused too? Katie and Tara and I need to...uh...uh ...

KATIE. *(jumping up)* Go brush our hair!

TARA. Yeah! Brush our hair! And powder our noses!

BETH. Oh. Well, all right, girls, but –

MEREDITH. Thanks, Mom.

(*MEREDITH, KATIE, and TARA hurriedly exit upstage center. TYLER raises his hand timidly.*)

JOHN. *(kindly)* Yes, Tyler.

TYLER. Um, Dad? I...um...I hafta, um...

(*TYLER leans over and whispers in JOHN's ear.*)

JOHN. Go right ahead.

(*TYLER exits upstage center. The adults all turn to look at LEXI.*)

LEXI. *(loudly; defensively)* What??? I was being *quiet*!!!

(*MEREDITH pokes her head in at upstage center, clears her throat, and gives LEXI a look.*)

Oh!

(turning to BETH)

Mom, I need to...uh, I need to...Bye!

(*LEXI jumps up and runs out upstage center. JOHN and BETH exchange knowing smiles and shake their heads. Oblivious to their exits, DAVEY is still merrily piling his plate high with food.*)

ERIN. Where are they all going?

JOHN. If I had to guess, I'd say it's time for *their* Thanksgiving good deed.

BETH. *(to* **JOHN***; rising) Speaking* of which…Honey? Could you give me a hand with something in the kitchen, please?

JOHN. Of course.

(**JOHN** *and* **BETH** *exit, stage left.* **PASTOR BRIAN** *and* **ERIN** *look at each other, amused.)*

PASTOR BRIAN. Do you get the sneaking suspicion, Miss Thompson, that we're in the midst of a setup here?

ERIN. *(laughing)* Funny you should mention it …

(**DAVEY** *sees an open seat at the end of the table, shrugs, and sits. He begins shoveling the food in noisily.* **PASTOR BRIAN** *and* **ERIN** *look at him.)*

PASTOR BRIAN. *(to* **ERIN***; eyeing* **DAVEY***)* Uh…you wouldn't happen to want to go for a walk, would you?

(**ERIN** *looks around at all the empty seats and then at* **DAVEY,** *who continues shoveling food into his mouth.)*

ERIN. You know…a walk would be nice.

(**PASTOR BRIAN** *and* **ERIN** *stand and move toward upstage center exit.)*

DAVEY. *(mouth full of food)* Hey! Where you all goin'?"

PASTOR BRIAN. Uh…out. For a little bit.

(**PASTOR BRIAN** *and* **ERIN** *exit.)*

DAVEY. *(with a shrug)* All right. More food for me!

(Lights fade.)

End of Scene

Scene Three

(SET: The Mastersons' barn; Thursday afternoon)

(Lights rise. The Masterson kids and **KATIE** *and* **TARA** *are sitting around the barn on hay bales looking glum.* **JD** *is sitting in the center. Everyone is silent. After a long moment,* **JD** *speaks.)*

JD. *(flatly)* I call this meeting of the Masterson kids to order.

(There is a long moment of silence.)

(to **KATIE***)*

Aren't you going to say "the Masterson kids and guests"?

KATIE. *(lackluster)* Oh. Yeah…And guests.

(There is a long moment of silence.)

TYLER. You guys? I don't feel so good.

LEXI. Me neither. I feel bad for Davey. His mom makes him eat a box!

KATIE. Not a box…box *potatoes.*

LEXI. Whatever. They still sound yucky.

TYLER. *(quietly)* He said he didn't even have a birthday. No birthday cake or candles or presents …

KATIE. That is so, so sad.

TARA. Poor Davey!

LEXI. He didn't even know what Christmas is!

JD. Well, to tell you the truth, I don't feel so good either. You guys –

KATIE. *(weakly)* And girls.

JD. *(smiling half-heartedly)* Right. You guys and girls…I think it's time to call off the anti-Davey campaign. Is everyone okay with that?

KATIE, TARA & LEXI. Yes.

TYLER. Uh-huh.

MEREDITH. I guess so.

JD. Good. Then there was one other thing I wanted to discuss. I think that, after all the mean things we've done, maybe we should try to think of something nice we could do for Davey.

MEREDITH. You mean, like an anti-anti-Davey campaign?

JD. Well…yeah. Sort of.

LEXI. *(jumping up)* Ooh! I know! Instead of dumping mashed potatoes on his head, we could dump a big bowl of chocolate pudding! I *love* chocolate pudding!

JD. Uh…well, Lexi, that's not exactly the kind of thing I had in mind.

TARA. Yeah. Davey might not *like* chocolate pudding.

LEXI. …Jell-O?

JD. How about if we stay away from the dumping-things-on-his-head idea? Anything else?

KATIE. We could always let him take Tyler outside with the slingshot again for target practice. He seemed to like that.

TYLER. *(whining)* Me??? Again?!? Why is it always *me*??

JD. I think maybe we should try to come up with something in which *no one* gets hurt.

KATIE. *(grumbling)* Okay. Fine. I guess no one in here has ever heard of taking one for the team.

JD. Any other ideas?

(The kids are quiet for a long moment. Then **TYLER** *hesitantly raises his hand.)*

Yes. Tyler. Do you have an idea?

*(***TYLER*** *nods, runs over to* **JD***, and whispers in his ear.)*

(jumping to his feet)

That's a fantastic idea, Tyler! Why didn't we think of that before??

(The other kids stand eagerly.)

KATIE. What? What is it?

JD. I'll tell you as soon as we get inside. I move that this meeting be adjourned!

(The kids move toward stage right exit.)

TARA. *(energetically)* And I second the motion!!

*(Surprised, the kids turn to look at **TARA**.)*

What? I've always wanted to do that.

JD. Come on!

*(The kids run out of the barn, stage right, **MEREDITH** in the rear. Just before **MEREDITH** exits, she hears **PASTOR BRIAN** and **ERIN** talking and laughing. She looks around quickly and then hides behind a hay bale at stage right. **PASTOR BRIAN** and **ERIN** enter the barn from downstage left.)*

PASTOR BRIAN. Okay, I've got one…Favorite season.

ERIN. Oh, autumn. Definitely. I love all the fall colors.

*(**ERIN** sits on a hay bale and **PASTOR BRIAN** joins her.)*

PASTOR BRIAN. Yeah. Me too. And it's football season.

ERIN. Oh, I know! Best time of the year, hands down.

PASTOR BRIAN. *(surprised)* You like football?

ERIN. Of course! I've always –

(playfully suspicious)

Wait a minute…Favorite NFL team.

PASTOR BRIAN. New England Patriots. No contest.

ERIN. *(with a laugh)* I agree. No contest. I mean, what other team has ever won three of the six Super Bowls they played in? Or scored more points in a single season?

PASTOR BRIAN. Wow. I don't think I've ever met a woman who actually knows her Patriot football!

ERIN. *(lightly)* Well…now you have. Okay. I've got another one.

PASTOR BRIAN. Shoot.

ERIN. Favorite holiday.

*(There is a moment's pause as **PASTOR BRIAN** smiles at **ERIN**.)*

PASTOR BRIAN. I'd have to say…this one. Definitely turning out to be this one.

(**PASTOR BRIAN** *and* **ERIN** *smile at one another. There is a long pause.*)

ERIN. *(embarrassed)* It's your turn. I've asked the last two.

PASTOR BRIAN. Oh. Okay…well, it's not really a likes-or-dislikes question, but…how old are you?

ERIN. *(laughing)* You can't ask a woman how *old* she is!

PASTOR BRIAN. *(playfully)* I just did! And now I think *you* have to answer the question, Miss Thompson!

ERIN. Fine. I'm not vain.…I'm twenty-nine.

PASTOR BRIAN. *(thoughtfully)* Twenty-nine. Hmmm….

ERIN. *(warily)* What?

PASTOR BRIAN. Oh, nothing. It's just…this little rhyme kinda popped into my head….

ERIN. It better have nothing to do with being over the hill!

PASTOR BRIAN. Nope. It was more like, "Twenty-nine and lookin' fine; will you be mine? – "

ERIN. *(teasingly)* "Hey, stay in line!"

PASTOR BRIAN. "Do you decline?"

ERIN. *(smiling)* That depends…How old are *you?*

PASTOR BRIAN. *(in a high-pitched, feminine voice)* Uh! You can't ask a *man* how old he is!

ERIN. *(playfully)* I just did! Now answer the question.

PASTOR BRIAN. Twenty-eight. I'm twenty-eight.

MEREDITH. *(in a loud screech)* Twenty-eight?!?!

(**MEREDITH** *stands up suddenly from behind the hay bale.* **PASTOR BRIAN** *and* **ERIN** *jump up and whirl around, surprised to see* **MEREDITH**.)

PASTOR BRIAN. Meredith?!

MEREDITH. You're twenty-*eight*??? That's, like…*ancient*! By the time I get through with high school, college, and medical school, you'll be…forty-three! That's older than my dad! I'm sorry, Pastor Brian, you're a nice guy and all, but I just can't marry you!

(turning to **ERIN**)

Miss Thompson?…You can have him!

(**MEREDITH** *hikes up her dress [she is wearing jeans underneath] and runs out of the barn, stage right.* **PASTOR BRIAN** *and* **ERIN** *laugh.*)

PASTOR BRIAN. Well, now that we have her permission... Would you care to come over for dinner and a football game Saturday night, Miss Thompson?

ERIN. I would be delighted, Pastor Brian.

(**PASTOR BRIAN** *offers* **ERIN** *his arm. She takes it and the two exit the barn, stage right.*)

(*Lights fade.*)

End of Scene

Scene Four

(SET: The Mastersons' dining room; Thursday afternoon)

*(Lights rise. **JOHN**, **BETH**, **PASTOR BRIAN**, and **ERIN** stand as couples in the dining room. **JOHN** is now dressed as a Pilgrim, and **PASTOR BRIAN** and **ERIN** are getting ready to leave.)*

BETH. So the two of you have a date Saturday night? That's *wonderful* news!

*(turning to **JOHN**)*

John, isn't that wonderful news?

JOHN. *(somberly)* Yes.

BETH. Well, it sure doesn't *look* like you think it's wonderful news.

JOHN. Beth, I am a Pilgrim. We are a very serious, sober-minded lot.

BETH. *(under her breath)* Yes, well, don't forget that half of you *died* after the first winter.

JOHN. Good point.

*(to **PASTOR BRIAN** and **ERIN**)*

A date?? Well! Isn't that splendid?

BETH. Yes. Who would have ever guessed that you two would hit it off so well?

*(**PASTOR BRIAN** and **ERIN** exchange glances and smiles.)*

ERIN. Oh, I think somebody here knew pretty well what she was doing all along.

PASTOR BRIAN. I agree.

*(**PASTOR BRIAN** and **ERIN** look at **BETH** knowingly.)*

PASTOR BRIAN & ERIN. Beth?

BETH. Oh, all right, fine. You caught me. But this is the absolute *last* time I'll play matchmaker. I promise.

JOHN. *(to **PASTOR BRIAN**)* Yes. So long as you don't kill Miss Thompson's cat, you two should be just fine.

ERIN. *(to* **BETH***)* Well, I really should be going. I need to get the girls home. Thank you so much for dinner; it was wonderful.

PASTOR BRIAN. Yes, thank you. The food was delicious.

BETH. Oh, we're so glad you both could come! And Erin, why don't you take the rest of your pumpkin pie home with you? I think there are still three or four more pieces...

(The adults turn toward the table. As they move, they reveal **DAVEY** *still sitting at the table, center stage. He is just about to dump the rest of the contents of a pie plate onto his dinner plate. He freezes and looks up at the adults sheepishly as they look at him.)*

DAVEY. Oh. Uh...sorry. Were you saving this?

ERIN. *(laughing)* It's okay, Davey. You can have it.

JOHN. You know, Davey, it *is* getting late. Maybe I should get you home too.

*(***JOHN** *looks around.)*

Hmm...I wonder where the kids have run off to this time. I thought they'd at least stick around to say good-bye.

BETH. I don't know. They did leave awfully fast after dinner.

DAVEY. *(with a shrug)* It's okay, Mr. M. They don't have to say good-bye. I can go now.

JD. *(offstage)* No! Wait!!

(The Masterson kids, **KATIE***, and* **TARA** *run in, stage left. They are all wearing their coats and carrying covered bowls and plastic bags laden down with food. The adults and* **DAVEY** *stare at them in surprise.)*

JOHN. JD? Meredith? Kids, what's all this?

JD. We're coming too! All of us!

MEREDITH. Yeah. Since Davey's family doesn't have a Thanksgiving, we want to take Thanksgiving to *them*!

*(***DAVEY** *stares at the kids in shock.)*

JOHN. Kids, that's a *great* idea!

BETH. So *that's* why you all ate so little at dinner!

LEXI. *(proudly)* We were *saving* it!

MEREDITH. And now we have lots of food for Davey's family. So can we get going??

TYLER. Yeah. I'm starving!

JOHN. *(laughing)* Of course we can go! We'll *all* go.

KATIE. *(to* **ERIN***)* Us too, Mom?

TARA. *(to* **ERIN***)* Yeah. Us, too?

ERIN. You bet. We'll follow right behind them.

(turning to **PASTOR BRIAN***)*

Would you like to ride with us, Pastor Brian?

PASTOR BRIAN. *(with a jovial shrug)* Sure. Why not?

*(***ERIN, PASTOR BRIAN, KATIE,** *and* **TARA** *exit together, downstage right.* **BETH** *watches them go and sighs.)*

BETH. They'll make a beautiful family, won't they?

JOHN. *Speaking* of family, maybe we should get Davey back to his?

BETH. Oh! Right. Come on, kids. Let's get going! It's time for another Thanksgiving good deed!

*(***BETH** *herds* **MEREDITH, TYLER,** *and* **LEXI** *off downstage right.* **JOHN** *looks over his shoulder at* **JD** *and* **DAVEY,** *who are still just standing around the table awkwardly, avoiding making eye contact with one another.)*

JOHN. You boys coming?

JD. Uh, yeah, Dad. In just a minute.

JOHN. All right. But you'd better hurry or you'll miss the boat!

(pretending to be a pilgrim again)

The Speedwell waits for no man!

*(***JOHN** *bounds off downstage right. There is a moment of awkward silence.* **DAVEY** *comes around the table and stands at downstage center with* **JD***.)*

DAVEY. Hey, uh…I just wanted to say…thanks, JD. This is nice…This is real nice of you.

JD. Aw, no big deal. I mean, after the way we treated you – hey. Wait a minute. JD! You called me JD!

DAVEY. Well, yeah. That is your name, isn't it?

(**DAVEY** *peers down at the bag* **JD** *is carrying.*)

So…what's in the bag?

(**JD** *lifts a bowl out of the plastic bag. He pries the lid off and peers in.*)

JD. Mashed potatoes.

DAVEY. Oh. Well, you know what you need with those mashed potatoes, right?

JD. What?

DAVEY. A little bit of gravy!

(**DAVEY** *lightly shoves* **JD**'s *head into the bowl of mashed potatoes, so that the tip of* **JD**'s *nose is covered with potatoes.* **DAVEY** *laughs and exits downstage right.*)

JD. *(shouting good-naturedly)* DAVEY!!!!!

(**JD** *runs off downstage right after* **DAVEY**.)

(Lights fade.)

End of Scene

End of Play

THE SET

Set instructions

Three simple sets are needed for this production:

Act I, Scene 1 and Act I, Scene 3 take place in Faith Baptist Church's foyer – a bare stage with a long pew bench or several chairs placed upstage. A small side table containing pamphlets or bulletins may also be placed beside the chairs, if desired.

Act I, Scene 2 and Act III, Scene 3 take place in the Mastersons' barn. The barn may be created on a stage left wing or on the extreme left of the stage. Hay bales should be placed around in a semicircle. Miscellaneous farm equipment may be added to the set as well. Actors may enter the barn from stage left or stage right.

The remaining scenes take place in the Mastersons' dining room. A long dining room table is placed at center stage, the edge of the table parallel to the edge of the stage. Eleven chairs and place settings are needed for the table, which should be covered by a long tablecloth. Actors enter the house from downstage right. There is an exit between the flats at upstage center leading into the woods and barn. The stage left exit leads to the kitchen, as well as to the rest of the house.

Lighting instructions

For the church foyer – bright, "fluorescent-style" lighting
For the barn – dimmer, outdoor lighting
For the dining room – normal indoor lighting

No spotlights are needed for this production unless desired.

PROPERTY LIST

Item	Act/Scene	Character Using
Tyler's dress shoe	Act I, Scene 1	Davey
Hay bales	Act I, Scene 2; Act III, Scene 3	SET
Ratty old baseball cap	Act I, Scene 3	JD
Long piece of twine	Act II, Scene 1	JD
Eleven plates	Act II, Scene 2	Beth
Eleven sets of silverware	Act II, Scene 2	Beth
Eleven drinking glasses	Act II, Scene 2	Beth
Eleven place cards with names	Act II, Scene 2	Beth
Thanksgiving decorations for the dinner table	Act II, Scene 2	Beth
Pumpkin pies (2)	Act II, Scene 2	Erin
Twine tied from chair leg to table leg	Act II, Scene 3	JD
Dining room rug	Act II, Scene 3	SET
Stack of napkins	Act II, Scene 3	Beth
Slingshot	Act II, Scene 3	JD
Plastic grocery bag with container of Cool Whip	Act II, Scene 3	Pastor Brian
Bowls/serving plates of Thanksgiving dinner food	Act III, Scene 2	SET
Dog food bowl	Act III, Scene 2	Davey
Large roasted turkey on a platter	Act III, Scene 2	John
Pie plate with 3-4 slices of pumpkin pie left	Act III, Scene 4	Davey
Plastic bags with bowls/containers of food	Act III, Scene 4	Kids
Jackets/coats	Act III, Scene 4	Kids
Bowl of mashed potatoes with lid	Act III, Scene 4	JD

COSTUMING LIST

CHARACTER	SCENE	COSTUME
Davey Bryant	Act I, Scene 1	Faded jeans and T-shirt
	Act I, Scene 3	Same jeans, different T-shirt
	Act II-III	Same jeans, different T-shirt
JD Masterson	Act I, Scene 1	Dress shirt, pants, shoes, and tie
	Act I, Scene 2	Same as previous without the tie
	Act I, Scene 3	Jeans, T-shirt, and ratty old baseball cap
	Act II, Scene 1	Pajamas
	Act II, Scenes 2-3, Act III	Jeans and button-down shirt
Meredith Masterson	Act I, Scene 1	Non-flowery skirt and polo shirt
	Act I, Scene 2	Same shirt; replace skirt with jeans
	Act I, Scene 3	Khaki pants and T-shirt
	Act II, Scene 1	Juvenile or Sporty Pajamas
	Act II, Scenes 2-3, Act III, Scenes 1-3	Long frilly Sunday dress (denim jeans underneath for Act III, Scene 3)
	Act III, Scene 4	Jeans and T-shirt or sports shirt
Tyler Masterson	Act I, Scene 1	Dress shirt, pants, shoes, and tie
	Act I, Scene 2	Same
	Act II, Scene 1	Pajamas
	Act II, Scenes 1-3, Act III	Khakis, button-down shirt with T-shirt underneath
Lexi Masterson	Act I, Scene 1	Brightly colored dress
	Act I, Scene 2	Same
	Act II, Scene 1	Pajamas and bunny slippers
	Act II, Scenes 2-3, Act III	Jeans and brightly colored shirt
John Masterson	Act I, Scene 1	Suit or sports coat and dress pants, dress shirt and shoes, and tie
	Act I, Scene 3	Khaki pants, button-down shirt, and sports coat
	Act II and Act III, Scene 1	Khaki pants and button-down shirt

CHARACTER	SCENE	COSTUME
	Act III, Scene 2	Turkey costume
	Act III, Scene 4	Pilgrim costume
Beth Masterson	Act I, Scene 1	Dressy skirt and shirt
	Act I, Scene 3	Less dressy skirt and shirt
	Acts II-III	Denim skirt and shirt
Erin Thompson	Act I, Scene 1	Feminine Sunday dress
	Act I, Scene 3	Denim or khaki skirt and pink shirt
	Acts II-III	Khaki pants and polo shirt
Katie Thompson	Act I, Scene 1	Flowery dress
	Act I, Scene 2	Same
	Act I, Scene 3	More casual skirt and shirt outfit
	Acts II-III	Khaki pants and a T-shirt
Tara Thompson	Act I, Scene 1	Flowery dress that complements Katie's
	Act I, Scene 2	Same
	Act I, Scene 3	More casual skirt and shirt outfit that complements Katie's
	Acts II-III	Khaki pants and a T-shirt in same color as Katie's only lighter
Pastor Brian Malone	Act I, Scene 3	Khaki pants, dress shirt, and suit coat
	Acts II-III	Khaki pants and button-down shirt
Mick	Act I, Scene 3	Khaki pants and polo shirt
Riley	Act I, Scene 3	If male – khaki pants and polo shirt;
		If female – denim skirt and polo shirt
FBC Members	Act I, Scene 1	Sunday dresses for the ladies; Suits for the men
	Act I, Scene 3	Skirts and blouses for the ladies; Khaki pants and button-down shirts for the men

OTHER TITLES AVAILABLE FROM SAMUEL FRENCH

DON'T KISS THAT PRINCE!

Megan Orr

2f, 3m, extras / Comedy, Jr. High/High School / Simple set

Prince Alan Alarming is in desperate need of an A in biology . . . and who better to help him than nerdy Princess Maria? But when the science fair comes up and Alan is completely unprepared, he sinks to a new low and weasels Maria's project away from her. The only problem—he's got to find a frog in time for the fair. (And Anytown's frog supply has been recently decimated by the kissing-frogs-to-get-princes fad.) It appears Prince Alan is doomed to failure—until a new scientific finding gives him hope. According to research, when a prince kisses a princess he doesn't really love, she turns into a frog! So once again, Alan goes to Maria for help . . . of a very different kind!

OTHER TITLES AVAILABLE FROM SAMUEL FRENCH

TWICE UPON A TIME

Megan Orr

3m, 4f / plus extras / Comedy, Jr. High/High School / Simple set

The title of Homecoming Queen is up for grabs and both Princess Aiden Alexander and Princess Christina Carlyle are vying for it. When Aiden finally wins the crown, she is thrilled—until she finds out that on the night of the big game, the Homecoming King and Queen must kiss. Now Aiden has to find a way to protect her horrible secret, the curse that has haunted her her entire life—if she kisses anyone who isn't "the One," he'll go into a 100-year coma!

Breinigsville, PA USA
16 September 2010
245538BV00004B/5/P